The
Carpet Mind

The
Carpet Mind

The Laws of Thinking Defined

Anthony Penderis

authorHOUSE®

AuthorHouse™ UK Ltd.
1663 Liberty Drive
Bloomington, IN 47403 USA
www.authorhouse.co.uk
Phone: 0800.197.4150

Published by AuthorHouse 11/18/2013

ISBN: 978-1-4918-8453-9 (sc)
ISBN: 978-1-4918-8454-6 (e)

Contents

Preface

While growing up in Southern Africa, continually exposed to farming communities and a great variety of animals in the wild, my brothers and I had the privilege of keeping an unusual collection of pets. Besides the regular dogs, birds, mice and meerkats, we also kept, much to my mother's horror, scorpions, spiders, snakes, lizards, and at one stage even a baboon.

This unfortunate creature used to provide us with hours of fun, as it was mostly at the receiving end of our taunts. The cruellest trick we played on the poor baboon was to pass it a paper bag with a rubber snake inside. On opening the bag it would faint on the spot. This, of course, I only learned years later, is a clever survival mechanism for its species. Baboons in the wild are forever in search of edible plant matter and insects and, therefore, often get confronted by snakes. Fainting protects them, as it makes them go limp and temporarily lifeless. Snakes only strike at moving objects.

What really got us rolling over was when we passed this baboon a mirror. Not only would it grimace and pull faces at its reflection, but it would also grapple with one hand behind the mirror, trying to touch this "other" baboon. It was clear that it could recognise another baboon on sight alone but did not understand a reflection of itself.

Trying to understand the human mind often makes me think of my childhood pet baboon, which simply could not comprehend its own reflection in a mirror. In our quest to conquer ravaging diseases and illnesses, the human race has made great strides in understanding the physical body. No other entity or subject on earth has been studied more intensively than our bodies. Yet, we are still not able to give a proper explanation of the thinking process, let alone present a definition of the conscious mind and our faculty of self-awareness.

Our inner dialogue, for instance, puzzles us. Why are we constantly having conversations with ourselves? Who is talking to whom in our minds? On top of this, there's the much-debated question of free will. Can human beings really decide for themselves? As we dig deeper into the human psyche, it appears that the answers to these questions are not at all that simple.

My childhood pet baboon with its mirror looms even larger when I attempt to understand the greater universe surrounding us. Sure, throw theories of relativity, the Big Bang, black holes, curved space, and antimatter at me, and I will concede that humans have come a long way since the days when we believed that the earth was flat and we were the centre of the universe. But there are troubling points underlying all these fascinating theories. What, for instance, was before the Big Bang? If the universe is expanding, what is it expanding into? Why is there something at all? No wonder Einstein exclaimed that the greatest theory still to be written is the one that will give us an explanation of physical reality.

But baboons and black holes aside, what would be the most logical way to approach finding explanations for the conscious mind and its thinking processes? I based my approach on two very simple premises, namely the Law of Causality and the Laws of Nature.

All scientific theory is based on cause and effect, which is also known as the Law of Causality. According to this law, all events are caused by other preceding events. Therefore, in our system of logic, nothing can happen by itself. This phenomenon is also subjected to certain principles or laws, which Newton and Einstein regularly referred to as the Laws of Nature.

It stands to reason then that even the process of thinking cannot happen by itself. It must be subjected to the Law of Causality, and, furthermore, be guided by certain Laws of Nature.

Using this as my guideline, I ended up defining ten such laws, or "Fundamentals of the Thinking Process", which culminates in my "Carpet Model of the Conscious Mind".

Throughout this book the reader will notice that I pointedly avoid using the term "consciousness" simply because I have a problem with its actual meaning; therefore, I stick to terms such as the "conscious mind" and "self-awareness". Furthermore, I use the term "non-conscious" for thinking processes we are not aware of and avoid words such as "unconscious" or "subconscious", which have too many misleading connotations.

Just about all of my conclusions are based on everyday experiences about which most readers will be familiar. I am not claiming that these fundamentals, or laws of thinking, are the final answer, because there could be deeper underlying principles of thinking yet to be discovered as we unravel the mechanics of the mind. Hopefully, it will help to solve many "psychological" problems and ultimately strip us from superstition about the thinking processes.

Chapter 1

TO SLICE AN ONION

During my childhood days I had to share many little tasks in the kitchen around dinnertime. Not voluntarily of course, but certainly through matriarchal insistence that evening is a time for the family to gather and share their trials and tribulations of the day. What better place than a kitchen while food is being prepared?

My brothers and I took on these tasks with great reluctance and muttering behind my mother's back since we much preferred to be outside at dusk—our favourite playing time—chasing imaginary beasts and fending off the enemies of this world. For this purpose we always kept a good selection of homemade wooden swords, bows, arrows, and spears at hand should the enemy suddenly strike. No plastic toys in those days.

The task we detested most in the kitchen was to peel and slice the onions for my mother's great variety of dishes because it always ended up a tearful exercise despite us trying out numerous remedies to stop our eyes from burning. But my painful encounters with onions as a child did not make me dislike them. One of nature's greatest gifts to cooking must certainly be the onion.

Apart from its diverse use in cooking, there are other reasons why I remember the onion so well. Just think what an onion's smell can conjure up in your mind: not only great meals ranging from simple fireside concoctions in the outdoors to gourmet creations but also warm and homely evenings with close friends and family or even romantic company.

And there's so much more to an onion. While you peel it, there's the colour and shape, which appeals to both the visual and touch senses. When slicing it, the sound of the knife as it cuts through the delicately folded layers will be followed by the fresh odour, which addresses both your hearing and smell senses; and then finally, there's the taste when you eat it. Depending on your background and experiences, this can make you reflect on a myriad of other associations. Then follows the tears, and what associations can tears bring?

It is clear that an onion can be remembered through the five traditional senses of sight, sound, touch, smell, and taste, plus a great variety of associations, which each one of these senses might produce. One can think of our memory of an onion as having almost uncountable tentacles of association reaching into the mind. It is no exaggeration to say that great chunks of your life could be recalled through an onion alone. This is why an onion presents such a good model of how the mind works in storing memory.

So let's do a mental experiment to test our memory of the onion. If we remove one of our traditional senses while we prepare an onion for cooking, where will that lead us? To remove sight would be the easiest. Try to peel and slice an onion in pitch darkness. The first thing that will probably happen is that you suddenly become wary of cutting your fingers in the dark. This will make your other senses sharpen up. You will now be acutely aware of your reliance on your other senses and how important sight is to you. But to slice an onion in the dark will bring even more associations into play. Apart from the fear of bloody fingers and experiencing it more intensely than ever before, yet another association has been created. This is the first time you have sliced an onion in the dark. In future, darkness can then also recall your memory of an onion.

If we shut down any of our other senses, similar associations will come into play. The one outstanding association will always be that you could not use one of these senses at the time. This then simply serves as yet another association added to your memory store of onions. But what would happen if we were able to shut down all our senses but one to experience an onion? Is it possible that there can be only one association attached to a bit of memory?

We do a mental experiment once again and allow only our sense of touch to operate. While you touch the onion you are now blind, deaf, and unable to smell or taste anything. How will your mind process this?

It would probably bring on the most unusual state of mind you have ever experienced. An onion never felt so strange! This will then become your association with this particular exercise, which highlights the concept of "state of mind", which is broadly the term used for how you feel or your emotional state at that particular moment. The association with state of mind then appears to be the one we will never be able to switch off—while we are thinking, at least. The mind, therefore, can never experience anything in isolation.

From these observations it appears that all our senses are at work while we have experiences, although not always as definitive as in the case of an onion. The mind, therefore, does not simply commit objects or facts to memory but rather our experiences of them. With this as background, I present my First Fundamental of the Thinking Process (FoT) as follows:

First FoT

All memories are stored with multiple tags of association.

Chapter 2

SLEEPING WITH ELLIS

Over the years it has happened to me a number of times that I would suddenly freeze in my tracks, struck by a thought, and then experience the awkward urge to walk backwards. This was normally triggered by a memory that hadn't occurred to me for a very long time—sometimes for decades. I'm giving my age away here, but it would have such vivid impact on me that I could not do anything but stall, trying to figure out the reason. Was it a glimpse or a whiff of something?

Out of sheer desperation I would then slowly walk backwards, sometimes in full public view, retracing my steps while I glanced around in a very puzzled way, hoping to find that cue again. Apart from probably convincing the onlookers that I was a complete weirdo, the exercise was mostly a waste of time as I was seldom successful. The fascination of the experience, however, was to discover all these amazing memories I still carried in my mind of which I was completely unaware: childhood friends, my favourite sweets, elated moments, sad events, and long-forgotten love affairs. They were all there, packed away in my mind waiting for something to unlock them.

So how do we remember things? Normally, we refer to something that reminds us of whatever we are thinking about at any given moment and accept it as the normal way the mind operates. It is only when we are struck by unusual and vivid memories, especially something we haven't thought about for a very long time, that their source can become puzzling. And what makes us remember certain things better than others?

While attending the anatomy course at medical school I, like thousands of students the world over, faced the ordeal of memorising all the anatomical facts about the human body. At the time, all of these were summarised in a small book called *Ellis's Anatomy*—a little monster containing some 50,000 facts of human anatomy. The professor of Anatomy assured us that if we knew the book by heart, we could pass the course.

"How can I memorise 50,000 facts?" one student cried out of sheer desperation during a lecture. "Sleep with it!" was the witty retort of another. Just about everyone fell over laughing. In a class full of young hormone-laden people, this was indeed a funny thing to say. What that student did not know was that he instinctively pointed out one of the fundamentals of retaining memory: emotional attachment.

Sleeping with 50,000 facts will take some doing, but the act of intimate contact is an emotionally charged affair we are bound to remember much longer than just dry anatomical facts. The same applies to any other experience and the facts surrounding it, whether it is a memorable scene in a movie, a heated debate, or receiving very good or bad news. When strong emotions are involved, we seem to remember things better. So why would that be?

Memory improvement techniques taught by mnemonics experts all have one thing in common: they are based on building numerous associations around any fact you wish to remember, sometimes with amazing results. These range from complicated techniques such as converting names into numbers, to making up rhymes or "hanging" new facts on familiar frameworks. This could be the route to your work, your garden, your lounge, or your office. Should you want to remember, say, the name of wartime poet Robert Graves you could think of a man who digs up a grave in your garden and who then removes a coffin. The coffin will remind you of war and the person "who robs the grave" becomes Robert Graves.

So, if many threads of association with stored memory make us remember things better, then the mind must spontaneously form even more threads of association with memory stored under emotionally charged circumstances. Obviously, things that stir emotions are more important to us whether it be for defensive reasons or for pleasure. The reason for this can be found in the known principles of evolution. Evolutionary forces made the act of copulation a pleasurable one, to be remembered well and to be repeated over and over again to ensure our survival through many offspring. If making love were as boring as washing the dishes or painting the house, we would not be here.

There is also ample evidence that even animals remember emotionally charged events better. In Africa's farming communities, for instance, it is a well-known fact that horses and dogs remember bad treatment just about for a lifetime. If a cruel owner inflicts pain on a dog or horse by beating it very badly, the animal will never forgive him. Their eternal dislike of the culprit is shown through cold behaviour and unwillingness to comply with any orders from that person.

I once spent a memorable two weeks with a team of herb harvesters in the Cederberg Mountain Range in the Western Cape Province of South Africa, which gave me some insight into the behaviour of donkeys. These harvesters and their donkeys trek up the mountains once a year to collect buchu, an herb used in a variety of medicines by the pharmaceutical industry. This herb only grows in the most remote and highest parts of the mountain range, which makes it quite a dangerous job, especially for the donkeys.

Sitting around the campfire at night talking to this unique band of men, I discovered that they knew donkeys and their habits very well. When the donkeys return, laden with huge bags of buchu, they need to find their way down many treacherous mountain paths back to the base camp where their loads would be transferred to trucks. It sometimes happens that a donkey slips and falls under the weight of the bags and gets badly injured. These donkey handlers assured me that when a donkey reaches a place where it was previously injured, even as long as two years on, it would simply freeze on the spot and refuse to move forward. Only by gentle coaxing do the handlers get the donkey past that point again. It's clear that even donkeys have strong emotions; and it certainly convinced me that they are not the stupid animals we generally believe them to be.

All of this points to the very fact that memory is evoked through association, but is it association alone? William James, the father of American psychology, devised a very simple but clever mental test more than 100 years ago to highlight the role of association, simply by asking someone to "think of something". The logical response might be "What must I think about?"—in other words, "Give me a cue".

These cues come in many forms. The obvious ones come through the five traditional senses. What you see, hear, smell, feel, or taste has a definitive effect on your train of thought. Sometimes, we also become aware of sensory input from internal sources affecting our thinking through stimuli such as stomach cramps, irregular heartbeat, breathing changes, low blood pressure, loss of balance, and the urge to urinate. Then there are the more subtle influences that operate through hormonal control. An overactive thyroid gland also known as hyperthyroidism is a force identified to affect thinking patterns, for one. Premenstrual syndrome (PMS) is also well known to affect thinking. Most women will attest to this.

It appears then that any sensory input, whether from an internal or external source, elicits a feeling or state of mind, which enables the mind to extract the memories associated with similar previous states of mind. Broadly, we think of our state of mind or feelings as the emotional value attached to that experience. How exactly this mechanism operates to find associated memories in the brain's maze of neurons still remains a mystery.

In summary, it appears then that a myriad of signals continually act on us through sensory input from internal and external sources adjusting our train of thought, while memory associated with the present experience is recalled. Using the above as background, and with deference to William James, I will therefore define my Second Fundamental of the Thinking Process as follows:

> **Second FoT**
>
> **Memory can only be retrieved through association with sensory cues.**

Chapter 3

TRAIN OF THOUGHT

As a kid I absolutely loved travelling by train especially on long overnight journeys. The excitement of travelling to a new destination, combined with the glorious smell of the steam engine and being gently nursed to sleep at night by the rhythmic clack of steel wheels on the tracks, made it a memorable experience every time.

My association with trains must be the reason why I arrived at the idea of equating the thinking process to a "train of thought". William James called it "streams of consciousness", which alludes to thinking being a continuous process gushing forward like a stream of water. I prefer my comparison to a train not only because we experience it as a continuous process but because it is also as unstoppable as a train, while at the same time, it regularly changes tracks to veer off in another direction. Should James have implied by "streams" that more than one thought could occupy our minds at the same time, he would have been technically incorrect. Your conscious mind can only be occupied with one stream or train of thought at any given time. I shall set out to prove this later.

But, what drives the thinking process forward, and what is the foundation that sustains it? To answer this question I shall have a look at a number of characteristics of thinking known to most of us. The process of memory storage and recall will be a good place to start. In the previous chapters, I pointed out with the definition of my First FoT that all memory is stored with multiple tags of association; and with my Second FoT, that memory can only be retrieved through association with sensory cues either from internal or external sources. I shall use both these fundamentals as a foundation for my next argument.

Using the analogy of the onion in memory storage again, imagine a certain sensory stimulus such as a smell which reminds you of an onion. Apart from the myriad of associations possible in the arena of food, it could also be an instant reminder that you are hungry, for instance. This association could then trail off into planning your next meal, which in turn can remind you of a venue for eating (which restaurant today?), your health (perhaps I am too overweight?), money (can I afford a restaurant?), plus a host of other things. Before long, your thinking could drift far off and end up with something that appears to be completely unrelated to where it originally started—the onion. While this process is in operation, we are also aware that any another sensory stimulus, something that you see, hear, smell, feel, or taste can sidetrack your thinking and set you off on yet another train of thought which could have absolutely nothing to do with onions or anything in the arena of food.

While you are bombarded with sensory input from your environment, you are also subjected to somatosensory inputs, which are the signals reporting the internal state of the body through sensations such as pain, pressure, balance, heat, and coldness, for instance, as I pointed out before. I shall simply refer to this as internal sensory input to differentiate from sensory input arriving through our traditionally defined five sensory organs. The feed from internal sensory input certainly has a definitive influence on our train of thought, especially when it becomes dominant. I am sure most readers will agree that this is how the thinking process broadly operates in the waking state.

As a train of thought proceeds in our minds, every new event experienced through sensory input is then simultaneously connected to past events by tags of association. This is how we recall memory as I pointed out with my First and Second FoTs. Here, another oddity about thinking reveals itself. The thinking process leaves a memory trace of its own operations. At a later stage we can recall the entire history of a particular train of thought with all the associations evoked by it. Our train seems to leave new tracks every time. I call this an oddity simply because there is so much we do not yet understand about thinking. Perhaps I should refer to it as phenomenal. The brain is, after all, an amazing organ.

But what is needed to keep the train going? What is the engine driving the process, and how is fuel provided? Neuroscientists tell us that electrochemical processes through the exchange of positive and negative ions are responsible for the transfer of information as well as memory storage in our nervous system. Surely any chemical process by way of exchanging positive or negative ions must itself run out of steam. A sensory stimulus, from one of the five traditional senses for instance, can get the thinking process going, but it should fizzle out after a certain amount of time. If this should be the case, what is the time span necessary between stimuli to keep thinking alive?

Brain imaging methods have improved dramatically over the last few decades and evidence from procedures such as EEG, PET, MEG, SPECT, and fMRI have helped enormously towards a better understanding of the brain. Unfortunately, none of these scanning methods are yet accurate enough to tell us the exact route of activation brought on by sensory stimuli, let alone the content of thought. What we see through most of the scans is the reaction of thousands if not millions of neurons at the same time. The scans also suggest that after a sensory stimulus fires the neurons, it dies down very quickly, sometimes in a matter of milliseconds. The question I am really asking here is: Does the brain need continuous or continual activation through sensory input to keep thinking alive? If it is the latter, then there must be a minimum time span between sensory stimuli to keep the thinking process going.

To illustrate this point further, let's have a look at a fairly simple animal—an ostrich. Ostriches are farmed extensively in South Africa, and I find it surprising that it is not a well-studied animal for a number of reasons. It is known as the land vertebra with the biggest eyes, nearly the same size as its brain. The size and bulginess of the eyes make perfect sense. It gives the ostrich practically a 360-degree view with a slight twist of the head. This combined with the advantage of the long neck gives the ostrich an edge on predators to use its powerful legs and speed to escape. The connection between such a small brain and those huge eyes must make fertile ground for many studies.

But the real reason why I bring the ostrich into discussion here concerns an interesting observation I made while visiting some of my ostrich farmer friends over the years. When the farmer wants to work with an ostrich—to pluck feathers for instance—a leather sock is put over its head, and it simply freezes. The ostrich will practically stand motionless for hours allowing workers to do anything with it.

The fact that the ostrich, normally a very attentive animal, suddenly does not know what to do when its main sensory organ is disabled could be the clue to the connection between the thinking process and sensory stimuli. If an ostrich gets just about paralysed by cutting off its sight, it implies that the brain needs at least regular sensory input to keep it going. I trust that sometime in the future neuroscientists will take a hard look at the connections between its brain and those amazing eyes. This might lead to more interesting conclusions regarding the thinking process.

Ostriches, by the way, do not bury their heads in the sand and then believe they are invisible. This myth is probably derived from their habit of putting the neck flat on the ground to hide from predators or conceal the location of the nests while keeping their eggs or chicks warm. It is, nevertheless, a handy saying to describe the activities of some humans in real life, especially in the world of politics.

At this stage, I need to point out that we are also thinking during the dreaming process but that it plays out somewhat differently to the thinking process during the waking state. What exactly fires the thinking process during the dreaming stage is not yet completely understood and to attempt a solution is certainly not within the scope of this book.

In summary then, the thinking experience appears to operate broadly like this: Sensory stimuli fire the thinking process, which rolls forward by feeding on memory recall and laying down new memory in the process. It is, therefore, safe to say that all memory is locked in sequence and that thinking is never static. We clearly do not think in freeze-frames. Neither are there gaps in thinking, nor can the thinking process come to an abrupt end while sensory input is sustained. One thought always leads to another. There is, therefore, no cul-de-sac to thinking, in the waking state at least. I will, therefore, stick to my unstoppable train of thought and define my Third Fundamental of the Thinking Process as follows:

Third FoT

The thinking process is sustained by sensory input and remains continuous in the waking state.

Chapter 4

THE CLEVER SHORTCUT

A distant cousin of ours, the chacma baboon, found in abundance in southern parts of Africa, uses a very effective system to warn of approaching danger by using sentries posted around the troop. These sentries—normally the older males—will be positioned on high ground or in trees at the outer perimeter of the troop wherever it is feeding, moving, or resting. As youngsters, we regarded it as a great challenge to see how close we could sneak up to a troop before a sentry spotted us. The instant a sentry saw us, it would bark and the troop would scatter.

This reminds me a lot of how our five traditional senses of sight, hearing, smell, touch, and taste operate. Before we allow anything close to, or inside our bodies, we rely heavily on these senses to evaluate the potential harmfulness of anything foreign to us. During the day we use mostly sight, while at night, mostly hearing, to judge things at a distance. As it gets closer, smell becomes more important, then touch, with the final scrutiny being through taste, should we want to eat it. Therefore, these five senses constitute our first line of defence. They are the sentries of the human being; firstly, to protect us against enemies or aid us in surviving any life-threatening circumstances; then, secondly, to find food; and finally, to procreate. Although I put food before sex, I am not denying that humans, at times, will go hungry in pursuit of a mating partner.

Apart from these five senses we also have a multitude of internal warning systems that can alert us when all is not well within the body. I mentioned internal or somatosensory input before, which can alert us to pain, pressure, heat, coldness, and so on. But there are also other messages flashing around the body, which we are unaware of most of the time. These are the signals controlling our vital functions such as heartbeat, breathing, blood pressure, and temperature control, which are necessary to maintain the equilibrium or homeostasis of the body. These signals normally follow predetermined neural or humoral pathways. The term "humoral" refers to body fluids of which blood is the best known. A great number of chemical substances, some of them called hormones, travel along the bloodstream to interact with cell receptors in various parts of the body, or they can be changed into neural signals predominantly in the region of the brain stem. Therefore, I shall use the term "predetermined messenger pathways" to denote the routes of these signals, which include either or both neural and humoral pathways. Only when some signals travelling along these predetermined messenger pathways break through certain threshold levels and effectively demand higher intervention by the mind, do we become aware of them.

Our vital functions need to be finely tuned to keep us alive. We simply would not be able to live if they were not constantly monitored and adjusted. I shall use temperature control as an example to explain how such a system operates. The human body is equipped with specialised nerve cells, which act as temperature sensors to keep our core temperature fixed at thirty-seven degrees centigrade. This is the optimum temperature necessary to maintain essential chemical functions that affect, inter alia, the pH and concentration of the blood. If the temperature of the body varies more than one degree, some enzymes in the bloodstream become dysfunctional and it could be dangerous to the body.

Through a feedback system via predetermined messenger pathways, the body automatically adjusts to maintain its core temperature. One of the crudest controls would be the process of shivering, which warms up the muscles when we are too cold. When it gets too hot, on the other hand, you could take on a red and flushed appearance simply because your veins open up and the heart pumps more blood to the affected areas to cool it down. In even more extreme heat, your pores would open up and you start sweating to cool the body down. Sweating can also be brought on by internal temperature increases triggered by high fever, or the intake of hot drinks, or a spicy Indian curry.

Imagine yourself to be in a fairly warm room where your body's temperature control system automatically adjusts without your awareness; then, the room heats up even more, which makes you sweat and suddenly you feel uncomfortable. This means that your instinctive ability to control temperature has reached its limits and your body is now demanding higher intervention. It effectively tells your mind to get involved and solve the problem. In other words, you are commanded to think about the problem.

Typical human reactions in such a situation would be to move away from the heat source, open the window, drink water, or switch on the air conditioner should any of these options be available. To do this, your mind has to tap into its memory banks and weigh up various solutions to its present problem. Should you have no memory of a solution in this particular case, you can still find it through the process of association, which I would like to explain with a practical example.

If, at this point you didn't possess the knowledge that drinking water is an effective way of cooling down the body, but there is a water tap in the room, how would you come to such a conclusion? You would now be in a state of extreme discomfort brought on by the heat with no obvious mechanical solutions, such as switching on an air conditioner, or opening a window to reduce the heat. Your mind will be racing around its memory banks trying to find an answer through association. You are desperate to cool down. One association that could spring to mind then is the opposite of heat, which obviously, is coldness. Your mind will grasp at anything to do with cold things, and depending on your past experiences, your association with cold things could include ice cream, snow, mountain streams, and cooling baths. Now a link starts to form in your mind between water and coldness. Then you spot the tap and suddenly jump to the solution of having a drink of water, and you dive for the tap—it's an eureka moment. You have now created your own solution through memory recall, feeding on association. This was then a conscious learning experience now committed to your memory. In future, you will always have this solution at the ready and consider a drink of water to cool down when necessary.

My first three Fundamentals of the Thinking Process form the basis of this solution. Your thinking process continued relentlessly driven by constant sensory input created by the abnormal heat (Third FoT); then you spotted the tap which was the cue (Second FoT) to form the association with water (First FoT). It's important to note here that the brain does not have ready-made solutions unless you've had previous experiences of similar situations. The brain, therefore, does not know more than us, but only comes to new conclusions through the process of association driven by sensory input. In short, we are not born with a great store of ready-made solutions.

We can assume that any living entity with a brain can get into life-threatening situations, of which it has no prior knowledge. Yet, through the power of association, it finds a solution, which points to a link between intelligence and the brain's ability to form associations. Intelligent minds certainly must have higher powers of association than non-intelligent minds. The speed at which these associations can be formed is obviously an integral part of intelligence especially for survival in life-threatening situations.

This, in turn, gives us yet another clue to the nature of the thinking process. It appears to be partly a mechanism that has the ability to fall back on experience by recalling memory through association generated by internal and external sensory input, then mobilise the whole system to its own advantage. Memory, therefore, can only have value if comparisons can be made between different bits of memory; otherwise, it would be useless. What we perceive as logic then appears to be partly a process of weighing up these different bits of memory activated by sensory input through the associations that link them. It is clear that the mind with the ability to store memory with multiple links of association could move forward in the struggle for survival.

But to get back to the matter of predetermined messenger pathways, how does the learning experience interact with the body or mind and especially memory storage? Most readers have had the experience of learning how to drive a car. Remember how awkward it felt at first to move your feet between the clutch, brake, and accelerator while you had to change the gears, hold the steering wheel, operate the indicators, and keep the car on the road? Now you do all of this without even thinking about it. How is this possible?

It appears that apart from the instinctive abilities we are born with, which operate along predetermined messenger pathways, we also have the ability to learn new things; and when repeated often enough, are relegated to predetermined messenger pathways. This means that we can perform repetitive acts without thinking about them at the same level as instinctive reactions. From an evolutionary point of view, this makes perfect sense for two reasons. The first one is our seemingly unrestricted ability to learn new things or acquire new skills. If we had to consciously think about every new thing we learned since birth every time we repeat it, we would only be able to do one thing at a time and completely neglect everything else while occupied with that particular action. We would appear to be stupid and slow. Driving a car would be impossible.

The second reason would be the so-called fight or flight reactions where adrenaline kicks in and there's literally no time to think about what we are actually doing. In the classic charging bull example of fight or flight, you are not going to ask yourself, "Should I jump over the fence to get out of the bull's way, or not?" You just jump! The same thing happens when you yank your hand away from a hot object, or blink your eyelids at anything approaching your face fast. You simply do not think about it and only become aware of the action after it has taken place. Instinctive reactions also imply the existence of predetermined messenger pathways to execute certain functions that do not require the intervention of a conscious decision. This clever shortcut system is not only an important survival mechanism in life-threatening situations but also appears to be the very tool that enables us to learn new things and adapt rapidly to fast-changing environments.

But what are the limits of the brain in creating new predetermined messenger pathways? I will use an example such as the act of typing, of which most of us are familiar. When we type, we do not think of the action of our fingers on the keyboard neither of the spelling of the word, unless of course you do not know how to spell it. By mastering the skill of typing, you must create a predetermined messenger pathway in your body for every word you know.

A transcription typist who types out court and parliamentary proceedings can type at the speed at which we talk. This is only possible if he or she has a predetermined messenger pathway for practically all English words in general usage. An average-educated, English-speaking person has a vocabulary of around 15,000 words. If a well-trained transcription typist can type all of these words without thinking about it, which is quite possible, this would then be the number of new predetermined messenger pathways or new instinctive routes that person has created in their body. And this has to do with the faculty of speech alone. Our capacity to create new predetermined messenger pathways that bypass the conscious thinking process is clearly immense.

All in all, it appears that we do not have to teach the body to create new messenger pathways, but that it happens automatically as long as the skills are repeated often enough. This then leads me to my Fourth Fundamental of the Thinking Process, which reads as follows:

Fourth FoT

The body spontaneously unburdens the conscious mind from continuous involvement in oft-repeated acquired skills.

Chapter 5

MEMORIES SHOULD FADE

Human beings seem to remember events well when it involves an intensely emotional experience especially when brought on by the element of shock. Many people, including myself, can still remember to this day what exactly we were doing when the news of September 11, 2001 broke. A testament to this is the yearly commemoration of this tragic event by a popular phone-in radio show in South Africa. Those who phone in are asked to relate exactly what they were doing when they saw television coverage on how the planes were deliberately crashed into the World Trade Centre in New York, killing thousands of people. It is absolutely amazing how many people still remember their doings at that moment seeing that the show is flooded with calls.

I pointed out in an earlier chapter that even animals such as horses, dogs, and donkeys remember physically painful events for a long time. Therefore, emotion also plays a role in memory storage in the animal kingdom. As suggested before, it appears that the mind forms additional tags of association with memory stored under emotionally charged circumstances. Obviously, things that stir up emotions are more important to us whether it be for defensive reasons or for pleasure and should, because of this fact, be better remembered. But how accurate is our memory recall and how well do we remember facts? The following examples will throw some light on this matter.

I once took a course in speech and drama where we did an interesting exercise in class to test our memory recall with the game nowadays called "Telephone" or "Whisper Down the Lane". The lecturer would line up, say, ten students and then whisper a short message to the one at the front. This student in turn had to whisper the same message again to the person behind him or her, and so on, until it reached the last one in the queue. The last student then repeated the message to the whole class. Compared to the original message of the teacher, which was written down beforehand, it always ended up ridiculously different. A simple sentence such as "Ten cows were grazing in the meadow and two went for a drink of water," could end up as, "Twenty crazy cows went swimming and two drowned." This clearly demonstrated to us the fallibility of human memory even with simple things.

Many of us pride ourselves on our ability to recall memory. Put your memory to a test and see how wrong you are. In the olden days, some memory could be recalled by way of photo albums or written letters; but nowadays, we have modern equipment such as voice and video recorders that can keep an accurate account of things that happened a long time ago. A good way to test one's memory is to think about a memorable scene in a movie you haven't seen for some time. Write down every detail you remember of a particular scene and then watch the movie again to check your facts. The chances are good that you will be very disappointed with the results because your mind will have warped your memory of the scene somewhat.

In the book *True Witness* by James M. Doyle, the writer, a veteran litigator, brings this very fact of our reliance on people's memories when they testify in court to the fore. He seriously questions the standard method of putting a suspect in a police line-up with other innocent people to be identified by an eyewitness to a crime scene. In the past, many courts have accepted this as enough evidence to find someone guilty as charged. With the help of DNA testing, it has been proved that even a rape victim who saw the face of her attacker could make a mistake and pick the wrong person in a police line-up. In this particular case, which the writer discusses in detail, a rape victim wrongly identified her attacker in a police line-up, which sent him to jail for life. He was exonerated through DNA testing after he had already served fifteen years in prison.

Doyle points out that many people could even have been wrongly executed in the past because of this practice. Other sources estimate that, until recently, courts in the US passed around 4,500 false convictions per year based on eyewitness testimony alone. Hopefully, courts will increasingly take note of this fallibility in human beings and look for more evidence than just an eyewitness account before judgment is passed.

What about an extreme example such as a person with a superhuman ability to remember things? In our recorded history there are many examples of people with astounding memories and I would like to discuss the well-documented case of the Solomon Shereshevskii.

Solomon was a Russian born in 1886, and his case study was recorded by the late A.R. Luria, professor at the University of Moscow, in his book *The Mind of a Mnemonist: A Little Book about a Vast Memory*. Professor Luria, a distinguished Soviet psychologist of his time, studied Solomon over many years and made some interesting observations during this period, notably that a phenomenal memory is not necessarily good all the time.

Solomon's unusual memory became public in 1905 when he started working as a journalist at a newspaper in Moscow. His editor noticed, much to his own irritation, that Solomon never took notes during meetings and interviews. When he confronted Solomon, he found out that it was not necessary. Solomon could remember everything in the smallest detail, regardless of how long ago it happened. Professor Luria tested him with long lists of numbers by reading it to him only once which Solomon repeated without hesitation and for good measure repeated the sequence backwards as well. This was an ongoing study and when the professor took out notes on subjects they had discussed fifteen years before, he discovered that Solomon still remembered them in exact detail. He had unlimited recall.

But everything was not plain sailing for Solomon. His vivid memory, which flooded his mind with images all the time, sometimes made him appear mentally slow. During a conversation, his mind could easily shoot off at a tangent as new words continually created new images. He struggled to forget things and could not forget painful experiences from his childhood, which remained as vivid as ever. Sometimes, he could not even get out of bed in the morning when the images of the day ahead became so powerful that he lived the day prior to its actual development.

Anyone who believed that they age gracefully would have found Solomon a disappointment. Meeting him for a second time in as little as six months onward, he would not recognise the same person because he claimed that the face and voice of that person had changed too much. His powerful memory made it unnecessary to rely on logic to remember things as any normal person would. When shown a list of figures in rows and columns with repeating patterns he would not spot the patterns. He simply remembered all the numbers because he could.

At the end of his days, when his mind started to go and Solomon ended up in an old-age home, his problem was slightly different from the memory loss the elderly normally suffer from. He still remembered a lot but could not distinguish whether something happened to him five minutes or five years before. In medical terms, Solomon suffered from a "grossly hypertrophied memory".

Professor Luria's observations give us some clues on how his subject's mind functioned. Solomon clearly relied heavily on visual memory as many of his remarks testify. It appears, however, that his mind spontaneously created an extensive network of associations around everything he experienced and involved more than one sense at a time. He remarked that once when he wanted to buy ice cream from a vendor, she answered in such a tone that, "A whole pile of coals and black cinders came bursting out of her mouth, and I couldn't bring myself to buy any ice cream after she had answered in that way."

It is now thought that he suffered from a neurological condition called synesthesia, where stimulation of one of the senses automatically results in the stimulation of one or more of another. In this condition, hearing a musical tone can produce a colour, or touching something produces a smell. Notables such as Franz Liszt, Edgar Allan Poe and Stevie Wonder were also victims of this, but they seemed to have applied it to their advantage in furthering their careers.

But why should the memories of ordinary people slowly fade away? What would be the evolutionary reason? A plausible explanation could be that it has something to do with our learning experience. If we were unable to forget past events, we would not be keen to learn new things, and in the process, also neglect our reasoning ability. In such a scenario, where everyone carried around masses of information with little reason for it, the development of the human race would have slowed down. Regurgitating facts from our past would have been one of our main occupations, as it was in the case of Solomon.

Our memories also need to fade if we want to have a normal life from an emotional point of view. If we were always to remember very bad news such as the death of a loved one as vividly as the day it happened, life would be torture. There is a lot of wisdom in the saying "time heals everything".

I trust that the reader has followed my reasoning up to this point and agrees with my Fifth Fundamental of the Thinking Process:

Fifth FoT

**Memory recall of past events increasingly
distorts with the lapse of time.**

Chapter 6

CLOCKS AND TAX COLLECTORS

Every year, normally during the same month, I land up at my office desk facing an annual obligation which I detest the most: filling out my tax return. As usual, I am late, and with the threat of penalties already hanging over my head you'll find me sweating away with formulas and calculations trying to figure out ways to give the taxman the least possible of my hard-earned income. I can remember this was always accompanied by our old-fashioned grandfather clock ticking away against the wall as a grim reminder that time was against me.

Doing all the calculations takes a lot of concentration but every now and then I find my attention drifts and I become aware of the ticking clock. As I proceed, and the realisation dawns on me that once again the receiver of revenue nailed me as he does every year, I find my blood pressure rising. A few minutes later, however, I am suddenly aware of the clock again.

So what makes me think of the tax collector and what makes me think of the clock? As stated in my Second FoT, we cannot think of anything unless it's triggered by a sensory cue. Initially, I could think of the clock through two different cues namely, sight and sound. It will drift back into my conscious mind if my eye catches it or I hear it ticking away. At this stage, another scenario starts to develop: I am building an association between tax collectors and clocks.

Anything that has to do with the tax forms can then also serve as potential cues to make me think of clocks again. These could be the tax forms through sight, my pencil through touch, and the beep of the calculator through hearing. On top of this, yet another association starts to develop in my agitated state of mind. My newly developed emotional state accompanied by high blood pressure and frustration now forms an association with clocks and tax collectors. If the experience is vivid enough, or repeated often enough, it can take a place in my long-term memory. From then on, a clock can trigger my unpleasant association either with tax collectors or high blood pressure. Clock makers the world over should please accept my apologies for this unfair association.

From this example a few things are obvious. The sound of the ticking clock is always there but I only hear it sometimes. However, while I am hearing the clock, I can still jot down figures and keep on writing. Is my conscious mind then involved in two actions at the same time? This is not the case as I pointed out before with the Fourth FoT. Acquired skills could be repeated without us being aware or conscious of it all the time through the creation of predetermined messenger pathways—in this case, for the act of writing. It is, therefore, not necessary to think about the writing for short intermittent periods.

Only when I start thinking about my writing will the ticking of the clock disappear once again. So it appears that we are capable of flicking our attention, awareness, or conscious thought between different points of focus, while other actions operating through predetermined messenger pathways continue seemingly unaided.

There are hordes of such examples that we are involved with in our daily lives. We have learned to do many new things through newly created predetermined messenger pathways while our conscious mind focuses on something else that is of immediate importance. I can ride a bicycle, eat an ice cream, and listen to music using my earphones all at the same time. This ability to do many things simultaneously is often referred to as multitasking. Some people are better at this than others and the mind's ability to alternate between different points of focus very fast creates the illusion of us being aware of many things at the same time.

In summary, it appears that one sensory cue takes predominance over all the others at any given time, depending on the need of the moment in the environment we find ourselves. This in turn provides the association to create the thought that occupies the conscious mind at that time.

With this as background, I would, therefore, like to define my Sixth Fundamental of the Thinking Process as follows:

Sixth FoT

The conscious mind can only be engaged in a single point of focus at any given time.

Chapter 7

OLD HABITS DIE HARD

I travel to work by car like millions of commuters all over the world. At the end of each working day I park the car in my garage, switch off the engine, remove the keys, lock the car, close the garage door, and put my car keys on a table in the entrance foyer in my house exactly where I will find them the next morning.

Then once in a while, as I'm about to leave the house early in the morning, and normally in a rush to avoid the peak-hour traffic, the keys are suddenly not in their usual place. With absolutely no idea where they could be, and me suspecting the early onset of Alzheimer's disease, a frantic search ensues, sometimes with the whole family taking part. Eventually, the keys will be found in a completely conspicuous spot where only I could have left them such as on the couch where I sat down to watch television the previous evening, or next to the kettle in the kitchen where I make my usual cup of coffee after work.

Many readers must have had experience of this with a wide variety of tasks which they perform regularly. Once in while you suddenly have no clue or memory of an essential detail you have repeated innumerable times. A good example would be losing your car in a big car park. We regularly see people searching for their cars in these car parks and I'm sure the majority of them do not suffer from Alzheimer's disease.

So which Fundamentals of the Thinking Process are at work here? I stated in the Fourth FoT that the body spontaneously creates predetermined messenger pathways with oft-repeated skills, which unburdens the conscious mind from continuous involvement in such tasks. My ritual of depositing my car keys in the same place has been relegated to this level and can then be practically done without thinking about the action.

But how could I then deposit the keys in a different place without remembering? Here the Sixth FoT kicks in, which states that the mind can only be engaged in a single point of focus at any given time. While I'm still holding the keys in my hand, I might suddenly be sidetracked by an event, which is not part of my key-depositing routine. I could be answering my mobile phone or suddenly get interested in something on the television while walking past. While still holding the keys in my hand, I now move to another location in the house. Remember, I can still deposit keys without thinking about it (Fourth FoT), and while I'm in a different location, I do exactly that while my mind is engaged with, say, a mobile phone conversation, or with something I am watching on the television screen.

The same mechanism is at work on the person who forgets where the car is parked in a large parking lot. If the person has parked a car hundreds if not thousands of times, the act of parking can be performed without thinking (Fourth FoT). Unfortunately, the location of the parking changes every time; and we all know that if we do not make a mental note of the parking spot, it is hard to find again.

While we go about our daily tasks, we, as humans, are mostly enmeshed in numerous events simultaneously such as talking, listening, writing, eating, or walking. At the same time, we are bombarded with the sensory feed from our surroundings through our five traditional senses. We could be buried under the facts emanating from our doings and our surroundings yet the mind appears to remember only certain things. Why would that be?

What about internal sensory input? There must be thousands upon thousands of messages continuously flashing through our messenger pathways to make our bodies function and keep us out of harm's way. How much of this information gets stored as memory then?

As long as the information stays trapped within predetermined messenger pathways, it does not make sense at all that this needs to be stored as memory for future use. Through our temperature control system, for instance, our bodies are aware of the surrounding temperature every single second of the day. But do we want to know about it all the time?

Our minds would be burdened with mountains of useless information if we had to remember every signal flashing through the predetermined messenger systems, whether from an internal or external source. Although we do not yet know the capacity of the brain as far as memory storage is concerned, it is inconceivable that there will be enough memory space to store the practically zillions upon zillions of information bits that have been running around in our predetermined messenger pathways since birth—let alone store them with tags of association.

The body's ability to create new predetermined messenger pathways within which regularly repeated signals from internal or external sources can be compressed, was evolution's way of protecting the brain from memory overload. All of this points to the fact that we need to be aware of something before we remember it. With this as background, I would like to define my Seventh Fundamental of the Thinking Process as follows:

> **Seventh FoT**
>
> **The experience of any event can only be committed to memory after conscious experience of such an event.**

Chapter 8

BABIES NEED TO CRY

The sound of a crying baby must be one of the best-understood signals emitted by a human being. Not only does it instantly alert us that something is wrong, but it also has the tendency to put us into a caring mood regardless of whether or not we are a parent.

Crying is just about the first thing a baby does when it exits the womb. It is clear that no one needs to teach a baby that. We are all born with this ability, which is very well applied throughout the infant stages mostly to signal hunger, pain, or discomfort. I can testify to this from the number of nights I was kept awake caring for my children when they were unwell. As we cannot imagine a baby being able to think about the act of crying, it is safe to say that the ability to cry is an instinctive or reflexive action operating through predetermined messenger pathways. Soon after birth a baby similarly demonstrates the ability to smile and chuckle when it is happy and comfortable. Tickling the baby or playing silly games with it easily brings on this reflex.

When we observe the acts of laughing and crying it is clear that these two extreme forms of emotion reflect our mental or physical state. If we equate crying to disapproval and laughing to approval, it points to the possibility that from an evolutionary point of view both these phenomena were one of a human's most important vehicles of communications before the advent of speech.

Showing approval or disapproval is observable in many other animal species although, not always as clearly as in the case of a human being. There is ample evidence that a sizeable number of animals such as dogs, cats, wolves, elephants, and gorillas display emotions akin to crying when they mourn their dead for instance. Whereas, they show the experience of pleasure or approval through frolicsome behaviour, which in turn, can be equated to laughter. Wolves of the Kalahari Desert perform a dance of joy after good rains. Bushmen who could eat practically anything to survive in hard times never touched wolves because they regarded their dance behaviour as too human-like. Darwin also pointed out that animals could clearly feel pleasure and pain and that the display of emotion is not the exclusive property of man.

Getting back to the human baby, it is easy to see why crying is an important survival mechanism. The baby cannot talk and has to indicate to the mother when it experiences any form of discomfort. Similarly, laughing, or actions closely associated such as gurgling, chuckling, or making pleasant-sounding noises, will reinforce the mother's good treatment of her baby. It helps to put her at ease and regain strength in her role as protector and provider.

So let's put emotions on an imaginary scale from negative to positive and position pain to the left, or negative side, and pleasure to the right, or positive side. We then further equate pain to punishment and pleasure to reward. The most visible way a human being displays the two extremes of punishment and reward will then be through crying and laughing respectively. Slightly inward on the negative side of the scale we can then position the display of less serious variants of the pain/punishment experience such as grimacing, sighing, frowning, or the sullen look normally associated with the state of depression. Similarly, on the positive side there is also a huge variety of the pleasure or reward experiences that are less intense than outright laughing such as giggling, smiling, smirking, and so on.

If we think of the extent of physical displays of human emotions that can be fitted into this scale, I am sure the reader will agree that it will be great in number. When we are worried, puzzled, or indecisive, it shows. When we know a person well, then something as simple as the shrug of a shoulder or the batting of an eyelid can give away the thought associated with that action. We regard this as non-verbal communication, broadly referred to as body language. Where these variants exactly fit into the pain or pleasure scale is a matter of debate and not necessary to go into for the sake of this argument.

Apart from an outward display of emotions by our bodies, there are, of course, also well-documented cases of inward displays of emotions not always visible to others. Certain thoughts can make your mouth go dry, create nausea or butterflies in your stomach, increase your heartbeat or even drop your blood pressure dramatically.

The display of emotions by the body obviously varies from person to person and also differs between cultures. People of Eastern origin are known to make less of a display of their emotions than Westerners. Their body language is much more subdued, but still present. One needs to know any culture foreign to their own fairly well before they will be able to make sense of the body language.

This brings me to the card game of poker, which gave rise to the term "poker face". To put on a poker face means that you deliberately hide your true feelings. It's essential in this game where a large part of the winning strategy relies on how well you bluff your opponents. When your hand of cards is very strong and you are confident of winning, you want to draw out your opponents to push up their bets. With a weak hand of cards you would want them to throw in their cards soon so that you can still win.

This is why top poker players are masters at the art of reading body language. Apart from facial expressions and simple gestures such as shifting around in your chair, fiddling with your clothes, or hands shaking nervously, even your tone of voice can give you away. Top poker players maintain that from the change in the size of the pupils in their opponent's eyes they can figure out the strength of their hand. No wonder many of them wear tinted glasses when they play the game.

What about telepathy then? Although many claims have been made that we are able to communicate through thought waves or have extrasensory perception (ESP), generally called telepathy, no substantial proof has ever been produced that this is true. In the context of the above it is easy to see how we can sometimes read each other's thoughts. By observing another person's body language, very similar thoughts are elicited in our own minds (Second FoT) simply because our bodies are conditioned largely to use the same mode of expression in the same environment or cultural milieu. Two people who lived together for a long time, such as a married couple, can easily read each other's thoughts. They have observed each other's body language in innumerable situations and know the thoughts associated with that very well. To outsiders they might appear to have a telepathic bond. This is why after many years of marriage you dare not lie to your spouse. Your spouse will immediately know when the physical manifestations of your real thoughts and your feeble explanations do not match.

When people communicate well, it implies that their body language is also in tune. We literally feed on the signals emitted by the body of the other person to keep our conversations going. Watch two people closely when they are conversing and you will soon come to the conclusion that our bodies are essential to convey the subtler meaning of words. When we laugh together, for instance, we get on well, but when a person folds his or her hands in front of the chest the conversation normally is not going well. A skilled orator who has the ability to work the crowd uses the collective body language of the audience to his or her own advantage.

I trust at this stage that the reader will agree that body language amounts to nothing more than the expression of the emotional value associated with our thought content. If the reader is not entirely convinced, I will throw in one more observation which is definitive proof that the emotional value associated with our thoughts plays out through our bodies. This has to do with erotic or sensual thoughts. Does anyone want to disagree that such thoughts can bring about extremely discernible changes in our bodies? I trust it is not necessary to go into any embarrassing detail about this little matter.

But is it possible that the body mirrors the emotional value associated with every single thought we have? Let me pose the inverse question: If the emotional value associated with some thoughts are mirrored by the body, then why not all, however subtle? It appears that the link between conscious thought and physical manifestation of the emotion associated with those thoughts operates as a reflex action along predetermined messenger pathways. We may be able to modify the physical expression of thought as the poker player does but not stop it. It does not make sense that the content of some thoughts have a physical link to the body and others not. I will, therefore, continue on the assumption that the emotional value associated with all thinking content has a physical link with the body and attempt to find a reason.

Let me get back to the crying baby and first distil the evolutionary principle present in this phenomenon further. Part of the theory of evolution proclaims that an entity could only go forward in the struggle for survival if systems were in place to cope with the demands of the moment. This implies that all systems present in living organisms are there for a reason.

For instance, we have two eyes to give us three-dimensional perspective. It enables us to judge the distance and the speed at which, our enemy or any potentially threatening object is approaching. This gives us time to prepare our defences or get out of the way. One-eyed humans would not have lasted long in a prehistoric world teeming with predators and continually being lashed by the elements and natural disasters.

Systems in our bodies, which are not in use any more slowly disappeared. A human does not have a tail because there is no use for it most probably since our ancestors started walking on two legs. When they emerged from the forests to carve out a living on the plains, a tail would have slowed them down when chasing prey on two feet. At the same time, it would have made them more vulnerable to predators who could grab them by the tail. On the other hand, a four-legged animal such as the cheetah uses its tail to act as a rudder at high speed when chasing its prey. Similarly, with most monkey and ape species, the tail has an important grabbing or balancing function simply because they mostly live in trees. In the case of a tree squirrel, it gives extra gliding length. Most animals still walking on four legs also use the tail as a fly swatter and it appears to have a function in the defecation process. The hippopotamus uses its tail to spread its faeces over a wide area when feeding on riverbanks at night.

So why did the forces of evolution provide us with the ability to cry? An entity such as a baby needs to be able to send signals for its own survival, and crying compensates for the inability to speak. The act of crying also conveys a sense of urgency, which can be further enhanced when accompanied by tears, a pained facial expression, and certain body postures. A caring mother can hardly ignore her baby when it experiences some discomfort.

It would be quite interesting to figure out why the acts of crying and excessive forms of laughter are accompanied by tears and why the two modes of expression are not the other way around. Why don't we cry when we are happy and laugh when we are in pain? I am sure the reasons can be found in the principles of evolution but will leave that discussion for another day.

With all the above as background, I would like to sum up as follows: Before the advent of speech, our thoughts were largely communicated through physical expression by the body and especially the emotional value associated with those thoughts. This is still observable in many animal species using partly sound, and partly body language, while lower species not capable of producing sound, rely entirely on bodily expression. A good example would be the mating dance found in anything from insects to mammals. Apart from elaborate displays to show their intention to mate, some species also change colours while they are on heat. The female genitalia of most monkey and baboon species go red and swollen while the male ostrich's beak and shins turn pinkish when they are ready to mate. The mating dance of the male ostrich is something to behold.

Humans rely mostly on speech to express their thoughts. It appears though that over and above speech, the link between thought content and physical expression, however subtle, has not been severed. It is also clear that the intensity of emotion associated with a thought also plays a role in the way it plays out in the body. There is a huge difference in the mere shrug of a shoulder when we simply brush off a thought and the poker player whose hands start shaking uncontrollably at the sight of an excellent hand of cards. Older memories also have a weaker display as time progresses. Thoughts, which could have driven us to tears at one stage, can simply be shrugged off years later. This supports my Fifth FoT, which states that memory recall of past events increasingly distorts with the lapse of time.

This phenomenon also partly explains the link between sensory input and memory retrieval as defined in my Second FoT. As trains of thought proceed in the conscious waking state driven by sensory input (Third FoT), new thoughts arise through threads of association with existing memory (Second FoT), which then appear to be simultaneously traced by the ancient expression of the body. Put in another way: the sensory signal elicits memory (the thought), which in turn rebounds and finds physical expression in the body. While the operating mechanism for finding memory is through sensory cues (Second FoT), it further implies that all memory must have a point of reference somewhere in the body. This could be a very important foundation upon which the brain evolved.

Therefore, I can only conclude that there is an irrevocable link between the operation of the conscious mind or thinking process and its physical expression in the human body and define my Eighth Fundamental of the Thinking Process as follows:

Eighth FoT

The body continuously manifests the emotional value associated with thought content.

Chapter 9

PAIN IS NECESSARY

Neuroscientists tell us that there are no nerve endings in the brain and, therefore, the brain itself has no feeling. But it does feel via the body through an extended network of nerve endings. How does the brain then decide whether something is either bad or good for us?

The answer to this could lie in our perception of pain. The experience of pain is still poorly understood but it can be broadly summed up as an alarm signal to warn us that something is either wrong for, or harmful to the body. The opposite of pain is pleasure. As before, I will equate pain to punishment and pleasure to reward for the purpose of this discussion. It is understandable that we would generally avoid punishment and rather strive for reward.

Children are taught the meaning of punishment versus reward at a very early age. Kids get a smack when they are naughty and sweets or praise when they do something well. This system is also applied in the animal world. Lions, dogs, and wolves nip their young ones as a form of punishment or alternatively lick or pass them food as reward. Even elephants smack their calves with their trunk when they step out of line.

Should we one day achieve the utopian state of a non-violent society where we do not smack our kids, have the death penalty completely abolished, and hopefully not kill and eat animals anymore, we still have to find ways to teach a value system. The modern trend is to educate kids by reinforcing good behaviour and withholding privileges for bad behaviour. "You cannot have an ice cream; go to the movies; or get that new toy if you don't behave," is the typical way kids are goaded into good behaviour these days. This, unfortunately, presents a bit of a predicament. Sending a kid to bed without food for bad behaviour, for instance, may be considered proper by some parents but it can be infinitely crueller than a good old-fashioned smack on the bum. I am not condoning corporal punishment, but when applied as shock treatment without inflicting physical damage, it works very well. Fortunately, moral judgement is not my territory, so let's return to the mechanics of the mind.

Kids are taught at an early age not to play with fires and naked flames because it is dangerous and can be harmful. Those who ignore this advice might push their luck until they have a bad and painful experience with the element of fire. The body gets punished, and from then on the child's memory of fire and flames will also carry an association of pain. This memory is not completely one-dimensional (First FoT), as the association with the burning flame could include extreme heat, flickering movement, the smell of the burning wood, the crackle of the fire, and in the worst case, the smell of seared flesh. Should the child experience any of these sensations through the other senses at a later stage, it could lead to the memory of this unpleasant experience with fire (Second FoT) and, therefore, act as a caution to him or her to avoid similar punishment to the body. This is most probably the reason why we have developed a warning system based on the colours red and orange to remind us of danger. Red flags, red traffic signals, and red and orange flashing lights can activate the association with fire or red glowing embers with its impending dangers and the possible outcome of punishment.

Most humans and even animals experience a low-spirited or depressed state of mind from time to time. When we feel depressed, the world around us becomes all doom and gloom. Whatever triggers our depression can set a train of thought in motion where we simply find the worst connection in everything. The essence of this seems to be a physical condition feeding on the mechanism of association (First FoT) through sensory cues (Second FoT). In a state of depression, the mind finds links to other memories that previously produced similar feelings. While we are spiralling down this seemingly bottomless pit of bad feelings, it can have a compounding effect that ultimately tricks the mind into believing that we can never escape. This could result in a nervous breakdown sometimes tragically ending in suicide.

So, why don't we like the feelings associated with the state of depression? Despite the many theories on the causes of depression, there is one fact we cannot escape. It causes a bad feeling, which sometimes points to a diffused pain spread all over the body. Whichever way we look at it, the state of depression sends a message to the mind through a mechanism akin to pain that it is a situation that should be avoided. Therefore, we are seemingly punished while the condition persists.

At the end of a hard working day most of us feel tired and slightly depressed. We then often have negative thoughts about what we are doing. Some of us might reason that it is a mental state. You had too much on your mind during your day at the office, or wherever, and it wore your body down. But does the mind really have anything to do with it? Let's consider an extreme example where you get worn down not by mental stress, but purely by physical stress.

A good example would be a marathon athlete. These athletes are trained to hammer their bodies for hours on end in their choice of a variety of popularised sports such as walking, running, swimming, cycling, kayaking, or cross-country skiing. Normally, when you are well-prepared and set off on this physical ordeal, you will be energised and in good spirits at the start of your marathon and look forward to the challenge.

But as time passes and the body takes a beating, your mental state also changes. Marathon athletes vow that they, too, go through periods of severe depression and mental torture. At the lowest point of physical depletion you are often struck by thoughts such as *why am I doing such a dumb thing?* or, *this is the last time for sure!* Unfortunately, copping out is the ultimate insult to the marathon athlete. Because of this, they will endure despite all the odds against them—even if they have to collapse on the finish line. That experience of relief at the finish is a very important driving force since it normally wipes out the state of depression instantly.

It appears then that both mental and physical processes can bring on states of depression. But why are we subjected to this? I can extend the question by asking, "Why do we have emotions at all?" A possible answer to this is that emotion, and by implication, the state of depression, is the yardstick of our pain versus pleasure experience endured, which then finds physical expression in the body (Eighth FoT).

Feeling good, energised, blissful, satisfied, fulfilled, exalted, and so on are all variants of the reward experience. Of all of these sensations, the human sexual orgasm can probably be considered as the most pleasurable feeling generated naturally by the body. Evolutionary forces ensured the survival of our species by not only rewarding the act of copulation with intense pleasure but also with an afterglow effect that could last a considerable period. And there is an added dimension to this: with the absence of sex, you are punished with feelings of frustration, aggression, insecurity, and intense longing, which are all variants of the pain or punishment experience.

When we fall in love with a member of the opposite sex, the object of our desire becomes an idealised figure we want to own, protect and spend all our time with. This points to a genetic blueprint which forces copulation on us through a complex reward-versus-punishment reflex. Although it has not been proved yet, I suspect that the act of copulation also involves hormonal exchange—hence, the afterglow. If this is not the case, we could have survived as a species on masturbation. Despite all the great words written about love, it could be nothing more than the body tricking the mind for the sake of procreation. Mother Nature was indeed clever to ensure the survival of her species.

If we equate our emotions once again to a scale where pain or punishment lies at the one end and pleasure or reward at the other, we can clearly see on which side the states of depression and sexual gratification respectively lie. In between, we have a huge spectrum of human emotions that produces varying fluctuations of good and bad feelings.

To illustrate the reward-versus-punishment reflex further, I would like to take another example which is part of the human condition none of us can escape: the message of death. Some time or other every one of us gets involved in a situation where we have to break the news of the death of a loved one to someone else.

I have had the unfortunate responsibility to deliver this message more than once. Each time as I walked up to the person, I realised instinctively that I was about to change the mental and physical condition of this person severely. One experience went like this: The brother of our trusted housekeeper died and her family asked me to convey the news to her. As I walked up to her, she could already read from my body language (Eighth FoT) that she was about to receive grave news and literary folded over before I uttered a word. When I relayed the news in the kindest words possible, her whole body went into convulsions and she started vomiting. After I helped to clean her up, she finally burst into tears.

And I have been on the receiving end of this myself. Once while on a business trip travelling through the beautiful wine lands of the Western Cape in South Africa, literally in a blissful state brought on by my magnificent surroundings, I received a call on my car phone that also instantly changed me. It was my mother who informed me that my brother's son—her eldest grandson—had died in a car accident. I distinctly remember that I could not get a word out for a considerable time while I just kept on driving. Needless to say, the landscape around me became totally meaningless. I finally got back to my senses and stuttered some condolences, but to this day cannot remember exactly what I said. My state of shock was so severe that it completely numbed my mind.

Many years down the line, it is relatively easy to take a hard clinical look at one's reactions under such trying circumstances. It certainly confirms my Eighth FoT, which states that the body manifests the emotional value associated with our thoughts. In this case, shocking news finds its expression in variants of the pain experience such as tears, convulsions, nausea, numbness, and so on. Life is our most precious possession so it makes sense that there will be an extended network of associations in our memory (First FoT) that the experience of death is the most severe punishment a human can endure.

In summary, it appears that the only way our minds know whether something is bad or good is through the pain-versus-pleasure experience of the body. Is the qualitative value of all our emotions then determined by a complex punishment-versus-reward reflex? If that should be the case, it implies that the human race's entire system of moral judgement is based on two extremely primitive foundations: pain and pleasure. Although many things point to this, I dare not present this as the final answer simply because that in itself is moral judgment, which is, as I have stated before, not my territory.

But how do we judge the qualitative value of something, which we have no experience of at all? We can come across many new experiences in our life cycle, of which we have no prior knowledge. The only way our brains can evaluate or assess such an ensuing experience is to compare it to the closest match with previous experiences (First FoT), which in turn will remind you (Eighth FoT) of the emotional value you attach to that particular experience. It is part of our survival mechanism that can warn us whether the ensuing experience could be potentially harmful or good. The hand of evolution is quite obvious here and once again points to the pain-versus-pleasure experience.

We are born with the ability to evaluate pain and pleasure but without any memory of what causes pain or pleasure. We need the body to make that judgment before we commit the association to memory. This gives me enough ammunition to present my Ninth Fundamental of the Thinking Process as follows:

Ninth FoT

Qualitative judgement of any experience is based on the body's sensory evaluation of such an experience.

Chapter 10

THE ACID TEST

Are we really at liberty to make free decisions, and can we ultimately be held responsible for our actions? These questions must be as old as humanity itself. While the philosophical doctrine of determinism dictates that there is no such thing as free will, existentialism on the other hand, holds exactly the opposite view.

Many great minds have debated the matter of free will over the last few centuries. During the 17th century, the great philosopher Baruch Spinoza flatly declared there is no such thing as free will. Other equally great minds took exactly the opposite point of view, such as the French philosopher Jean-Paul Sartre, known for his existentialist view of life. Sartre regarded man as a free agent burdened with decisions.

It is interesting to note that the scholars of Shakespeare agree that the great bard also questioned free will. In many of his plays he alludes in one way or another to an external power being responsible for the script of life. In the oration by Jacques, one of the characters in his play *As You Like It*, he comes closest to outright admission of it in those famous lines: "All the world's a stage, and all the men and women merely players . . ."

Why do people generally have resistance against the notion that we possibly live in a world where there is no free will? One reason is certainly that it would imply that criminals are not accountable for their actions. However, the fact that the courts of nearly all the world's judicial systems allow mitigating circumstances to be considered before verdict is passed, is our way of conceding that humans have, at least under certain circumstances, no free will and could not always be held responsible for their actions.

It is especially the gatekeepers of the religious fraternity who are vehemently against the notion of *no* free will. Being able to exercise free will is seen as the basis of human morality. The belief that humans are free to decide whether they want to land up in heaven or hell one day is the foundation of all mainstream religious movements. Religious people also believe that living a good life on earth in accordance with their scriptural guidelines ensures the blessings of their god on a day-to-day basis. They, therefore, regularly pray to their gods to seek a favourable outcome of their future endeavours.

Should it be proved, as I set out to do in this chapter, that there is no such thing as free will, it implies that all future events including our thinking processes are pre-determined and unchangeable. An entity such as a god would then continually have to tamper with the laws of nature to influence the outcome of future events, which will make the universe chaotic and impossible. Therefore, a god has no function in our universe.

It is significant that the debate around free will has now progressed from the arena of the philosopher to that of the neuroscientist with the introduction of the concept called "readiness potential" (RP). This term was first introduced as "Bereitshaftspotential" by the German neurologist Hans Kornhuber and his postgraduate student Lüder Deecke in 1964, and more fully, one year later. A few years later, Benjamin Libet and other researchers confirmed this in numerous subsequent papers. Through EEG monitoring, these researchers have found that conscious decision for voluntary action lags 350 milliseconds or more behind a negative event-related or "readiness potential" spread over wide areas of the brain. Therefore, one's RP suggests that we only become consciously aware of seemingly voluntary actions after the brain has already taken the decision. This finding seriously challenges free will from a scientific point of view.

But what would really prove that a human being is capable of independent decision-making or exercising free will? What is the acid test? Surely, that would be the ability to make a random decision. Such a decision implies that it is unbiased and external forces play no role in the choice. But what does the concept of randomness imply?

Rolling a dice, for instance, which could land up with any number from one to six at the top, would be a good example of a random outcome. We can safely say that any number from one to six has an equal chance or probability of showing up. But, statisticians tell us, if you throw the dice a great number of times, all the numbers will eventually come up the same number of times. This has actually been proved by rolling the dice thousands of times. Pity the poor man's wrists that did that job!

With the advance of the computer, the dice has been replaced by the Random Number Generator, which is regularly used in cryptography, statistical sampling, gambling, and computer games. Computer boffins and statisticians assure us that this little tool is totally unbiased in its choice within certain parameters. Given enough time though, we're still stuck with the same predicament as with the dice: the computer will eventually end up selecting its available choices the same number of times. So, if you are a gambler with a good supply of cash playing a game of chance and you live long enough, you will end up with the same amount of money with which you started. Wise gamblers obviously step out of the game at the crest of their winnings, but in most cases their cash does not last long enough.

From a mathematical point of view, I would like to sum up this phenomenon as follows: The degree of randomness for any eventuality is inversely proportional to time. Therefore, given enough time, there is, strictly speaking, no such thing as randomness. This highlights the inherent contradiction in the concept of randomness and agrees with the determinist point of view that there is no such thing as randomness. But what's all of this got to do with thinking?

Well, if we roll the dice once, or activate a random number on a computer only once, then certainly time is not a factor, and the outcome would be the closest to what we consider as truly an unbiased one. Unless someone else comes up with a better way of testing free choice, we're stuck with this one. But can the mind match this?

I suggest a simple mental experiment where we ask you to choose any number from one to ten. This is certainly one of the most reasonable and unemotional tests you can be subjected to, especially if there's no reward or punishment attached to your choice. Just simply choose a number. If you could prove that your choice was unbiased and totally free from external influence, then certainly the human mind is capable of exercising the option of free choice.

Okay, so you have chosen a number and we are going to test your choice. Let's first look at a typical crude control that could have influenced your choice. If, say, you have chosen eight just because you believe people generally choose threes, sevens, fives, and so on, and you just wanted to be different, then you have already fallen into the trap. Your memory of association with number choices has been revived, which exposed your bias and influenced your decision. You were, therefore, steered by external forces. It is clearly not a free choice then.

So let's refine the exercise. Empty your mind completely of what you believe to be external influences. Just pick a number. Do not include reason. Reasoning means applying logic and that implies weighing up external forces. Applying logic is, therefore, the furthest you can be from exercising free choice. Another way of doing it would be, for instance, to think of a tranquil pool with the numbers one to ten floating in it. You are simply going to put out your imaginary hand and fish out one of them. But, unfortunately thinking does not operate like this. You have to decide!

But before you make your "unbiased" decision, we must first investigate how your memory of numbers came about. At this point, I have to remind you of my memory model of the onion, my First FoT, which states that "all memories are stored with multiple tags of association," and my Second FoT, which states that "memory can only be retrieved through association with sensory cues."

Just as your memory of an onion has many tentacles of association stretching into your mind, the same can be said of numbers. Every experience you have had of numbers will have tags of association linking it to other associations in your mind. Obviously, the associations with numbers might not be as pronounced, as in the case of an onion, but there will nevertheless be some, because nothing can be experienced in isolation, as stated before. All your memories of numbers are, therefore, hardly floating in a tranquil pool. They are more likely trapped in an intricate web with numerous threads of association attached to them, all ultimately linked to your emotions, feelings, or state of mind when you last experienced them.

So, while you are now under the pressure to make a choice, the numbers one to ten will continually bob up and down from various locations of association to occupy your conscious mind. Here, once again, I have to remind you of yet another one of my fundamentals operating. Namely, the Third FoT, which states "the thinking process is sustained by sensory input and remains continuous in the waking state." Therefore, you cannot stop or control the bombardment of sensory feeds and at the moment of your choice, you will merely pick the number linked to the association revived by your last dominant sensory cue. Your predominant sensory feed at the very instant of your choice is the one that picks the number (Second FoT). You only become conscious of this after the choice has been made.

Another factor that needs consideration here and which certainly strengthens my argument is the Law of Causality. This law dictates that within the universe in which we live, nothing can happen by itself. For every effect there has to be a cause. Our world is causally closed. From this consideration alone it seems impossible that a choice can be made without a reason or cause.

In the conscious state we are aware that most of the time various options exist to solve any problem facing us. As soon as we apply what we call logic we are conceding that there are forces influencing our choice. This perceived ability to exercise the option of choice then creates the illusion of free will. We should also not forget that the options themselves are also forced upon us, which in the first place, means that our choices cannot be free anyway.

From this, I can only conclude that it is impossible to exercise any free option of choice and I call it my Tenth Fundamental of the Thinking Process defined as follows:

Tenth FoT

The human mind is devoid of exercising free choice.

Chapter 11

CARPET MIND

Who couldn't admire a good Persian carpet? Upon closer inspection of such a carpet, one might get a glimpse of the human toil that went into producing a typical masterpiece. In a true Persian, every knot in the tightly packed pile is tied by hand in a myriad of colours and intriguing patterns to represent the memories of generation upon generation of carpet makers. No wonder many of these magnificent creations are considered pure works of art.

I would like to equate the human mind to a Persian carpet as a stepping stone towards a better understanding of our thinking processes. Just as the mind has a physical foundation in terms of neurons, dendrites, synapses, and blood vessels, a Persian consists of different coloured knots of either wool or silk woven into a mesh-like base called warps and wefts that you ultimately cannot see. This base is necessary to sustain the shape and final appearance of the carpet just as the physical parts of our brain support the thinking process.

Imagine then that each single-coloured knot tied into the base of the carpet represents a memory trace in the brain. In the carpet, these knots are arranged into different coloured patches and patterns that we can equate to areas of associated memories, just as it is arranged in the brain. Neuroscientists have already mapped large parts of the brain associated with similar experiences and functions such as sight, hearing, smell, various types of feelings, and so on. Each colour patch in the carpet consisting of hundreds, if not thousands, of tightly packed-together knots, can represent memory clusters of similar objects, experiences, and sensations.

Our experience of an onion, as explained in my memory model of an onion, can then be represented in at least seven clusters. These will be the association with the five traditional senses: the act of crying (if onions ever brought tears to your eyes) and your state of mind, mood, or feelings at the time when you experienced it. Your memory of an onion is, therefore, positioned at various locations in our carpet model. When the memory of an onion is evoked through a sensory cue (Second FoT) within one of these patches, it can also form links to the other patches, thereby reminding you of the other characteristics of an onion, or various associated experiences. This implies that all the clusters in the carpet must be linked to others associated with them. We should then further imagine an invisible mesh of interconnecting fibres underneath the visible surface of the carpet connecting the various clusters just like synapses in the brain are the connections between neurons. Ultimately, all clusters are connected with one another via other clusters. These never-ending links between the clusters via their strands make it possible for the thinking process in the waking state to stay in a state of continuous flux and never come to a dead end (Third FoT).

The connections between our memories of the experience of any event will stretch like tentacles below the surface of the carpet reaching into its various patches of association. This explains the phenomena of a partly damaged brain that can still recall the memory of a variety of experiences. It would not be possible if the memory of an experience was stored in one patch only. Should that patch be damaged, all the memory of that experience would be completely obliterated. Somehow, evolution managed a mechanism for the survival of some memory even when the brain gets partly damaged through disease or accidents.

If we look at the carpet from a distance, we will also notice that apart from clusters organised in various sizes and colours, they themselves are, in turn, organised in bigger patterns. The bigger patterns also have similar characteristics at yet another level. We can easily think of all the smell clusters representing a variety of smell experiences closely tucked together because they share the smell associations. Similarly, there are other patches of clusters representing various experiences of sight, hearing, touch, good feelings, bad feelings, heat, coldness, etc. We don't know yet on how many levels the brain forms associations between the memories of different events, but it will not be an exaggeration to imagine them to be myriads upon myriads in number seeing that there are trillions of neurons in the brain.

The bigger patterns on the carpet are, in turn, part of even bigger arrangements that, in total, represent all your memory. Each carpet has its own distinctive look and feel just as every person has his or her own unique personality. The appearance of the entire carpet can, therefore, be equated to your personality. If a person is a very moody type, often inclined to collapse into bouts of depression, and we equate bad mood and depression to dark colours, then that carpet will have a predominance of dark patches giving it a generally sombre look. A person with a sunny disposition can be thought of as one with many light and colourful patches; whereas a temperamental and impulsive person will have many different colour patches not completely fitting together.

Our brains are bombarded with sensory input all the time during the waking state. We continuously smell, see, hear, taste, or feel things, but don't think about it all the time. Similarly, our somatosensory input representing a mass of information from internal sources such as temperature, blood pressure, heart beat, breathing, and hormonal balance feeds into our brain, but we only become aware of it should it exceed the threshold levels of our predetermined pathways. Broadly, we can also refer to these as our non-conscious experiences that never stop. This sensory feed does not represent thinking or the conscious mind, since we are not aware of it. We can think of this information as running around in the interconnecting mesh underneath the surface of the carpet.

When sensory input jumps beyond the threshold of the predetermined messenger pathways into our conscious mind, it activates some memory strands in the pile of the carpet causing it to move. The moving strand then represents our conscious experience at the time and the elicited memory associated with that experience. The moving strands, in turn, cause other strands nearby, or even in other patches, to move due to their interconnectivity as explained before. Every time the strand moves, we can also think of its colour changing slightly due to the memory of the current experience written or stored over previous experiences. This alters the connections or association of that experience somewhat and could partly be the reason why memory recall of events distorts over time (Fifth FoT).

In total, it would give the appearance of a wave running through a particular patch. The wave can suddenly disappear and then reappear at another patch just as our attention or train of thought shifts to another point of focus driven by sensory input in the waking state (Sixth FoT). Think of a breeze blowing over a wheat field touching clusters of individual plants in different patches that gives the appearance of waves running through them. The crest of this wave, driven by an invisible "sensory breeze", then represents the focal point of our conscious thinking process. From the perspective of this model, our conscious mind then behaves like a wave, which resonates with its environment through the body as conduit.

This carpet model then explains a number of aspects about the thinking process and practically all of my Fundamentals of the Thinking Process, which I would like to summarise as follows:

First FoT: All memories are stored with multiple tags of association.

Carpet Model: The mesh of fibres underneath the carpet's pile, link the memory strands in various areas to other patches of association. Therefore, the memory of any event is not stored in one location only.

Second FoT: Memory can only be retrieved through association with sensory cues.

Carpet Model: Memory is only evoked when the strands move, which implies that it needs to be activated by sensory input before it becomes a conscious experience.

Third FoT: The thinking process is sustained by sensory input and remains continuous in the waking state.

Carpet Model: Thinking, represented as a wave running through the carpet, is never static and remains in flux driven by the "sensory breeze". The conscious mind represented by the thinking process can further only erupt when sensory input exceeds the limits of predetermined messenger pathways.

Fourth FoT: The body spontaneously unburdens the conscious mind from continuous involvement in oft-repeated acquired skills.

Carpet Model: When tasks or newly acquired skills are repeated often enough, new self-functioning pathways are created in the mesh underneath the surface of the carpet. Therefore, they become invisible and not part of the conscious experience.

Fifth FoT: Memory recall of past events increasingly distorts with the lapse of time.

Carpet Model: The "sensory breeze" continuously adds memory of new conscious experiences by changing the colour of the strands somewhat. New associations are partly stored over older ones, and possibly alter their connections. This could be the reason why older memories get more and more distorted.

Sixth FoT: The conscious mind can only be engaged in a single point of focus at any given time.

Carpet Model:	Only one wave runs through the carpet at any given time continually changing its location as it finds new links of association and jumps to other patches. The crest of the wave represents the point of mental focus. There can only be one wave at a time.
Seventh FoT:	The experience of any event can only be committed to memory after conscious experience of such an event.
Carpet Model:	New memory is only added when the sensory breeze activates the strands in the pile to move, which effectively is the conscious mind getting involved.
Eighth FoT:	The body continuously manifests the emotional value assigned to thought content.
Carpet Model:	The wave representing the conscious mind is produced by physical means just as the body is the conduit of all sensory input. When existing memory is evoked its previous physical connection with the body is manifested.
Ninth FoT:	Qualitative judgement of an experience is based on the body's sensory evaluation of such an experience.
Carpet Model:	The body is the only conduit of sensory input and the evaluation of any experience is, therefore, dependent upon which patch the body associates such an experience.
Tenth FoT:	The human mind is devoid of exercising free choice.
Carpet Model:	With no "sensory breeze" there is no wave present in the model. Decision-making is, therefore, dependent on the sensory feed at any given moment, which in turn determines the position of the crest of the wave.

All in all, my Carpet Model explains how the thinking process operates through a constant rebuilding of associations with existing memory driven by sensory input; while new memory is laid down in the process. I trust that this model will help the reader to understand the conscious mind or thinking process somewhat better, or inspire someone to produce an even better model.

Addenda

FUNDAMENTALS OF THE THINKING PROCESS (FoT)

First FoT: All memories are stored with multiple tags of association.

Second FoT: Memory can only be retrieved through association with sensory cues.

Third FoT: The thinking process is sustained by sensory input and remains continuous in the waking state.

Fourth FoT: The body spontaneously unburdens the conscious mind from continuous involvement in oft-repeated acquired skills.

Fifth FoT: Memory recall of past events increasingly distorts with the lapse of time.

Sixth FoT: The conscious mind can only be engaged in a single point of focus at any given time.

Seventh FoT: The experience of an event can only be committed to memory after conscious experience of such an event.

Eighth FoT: The body continuously manifests the emotional value assigned to thought content.

Ninth FoT: Qualitative judgement of any experience is based on the body's sensory evaluation of such an experience.

Tenth FoT: The human mind is devoid of exercising free choice.

The author with a poster of his first attempt to define some
Fundamentals of the Thinking Process as on 3 March 2007

Bibliography

baboon. (2009). In *Encyclopædia Britannica*. Retrieved 27 October 2009, from Encyclopædia Britannica Online:
http://www.britannica.com/EBchecked/topic/47496/baboon

Bowlby, J. (1961). *Processes of Mourning, Int. J. Psycho-Anal,* 42:317-340, http://www.pep-web.org/document.php?id=ijp.042.0317a

Caro, M. (1994) *The Body Language of Poker: Mike Caro's Book of Tells*. Las Vegas: Cardoza Publishing.

Christos, G. A. (1996). Investigation of the Crick-Mitchisgrvon reverse-learning dream sleep hypothesis in a dynamical setting. *Neural Networks*, 9, 427-434

Colman, A. M., (2006). *Oxford Dictionary of Psychology*. New York: Oxford University Press, Inc.

Crick, F. & Mitchison, G. (1983). The Function of Dream Sleep. *Nature*, 304, 113-114.

Crowell, S. (2009). "Existentialism". *The Stanford Encyclopedia of Philosophy (Winter 2009 Edition)*, Edward N. Zalta(ed.), http://plato.stanford.edu/archives/win2009/entries/existentialism/

Damasio, A. (1999). *The Feeling of What Happens.* San Diego: Harcourt.

Dawkins, R. (2009). *The Greatest Show on Earth: The Evidence for Evolution.* London: Transworld Publishers (Random House).

Deecke, L., & Sheid, P., Kornhuber, H. H. (1969). Distribution of readiness potential, pre-motion positivity, and motor potential of the human cerebral cortex preceding voluntary finger movements. *Experimental Brain Research, 7/2,* 158-168.

Dennett, D. C. (1986). *Content and Consciousness.* New York: Routledge.

depression. (2010). In *Encyclopædia Britannica.* Retrieved 4 January 2010, from Encyclopædia Britannica Online: http://www.britannica.com/EBchecked/topic/158349/depression

Descartes, R. (2010). In *Encyclopædia Britannica.* Retrieved 11 January 2010, from Encyclopædia Britannica Online: http://www.britannica.com/EBchecked/topic/158787/Rene-Descartes

Doyle, J. M. (2005). *True Witness.* New York: Palgrave Macmillan.

dream. (2009). In *Encyclopædia Britannica.* Retrieved 10 and 23 November 2009, from Encyclopædia Britannica Online: http://www.britannica.com/EBchecked/topic/171188/dream

emotion. (2009). In *Encyclopædia Britannica.* Retrieved 21 October 2009, from Encyclopædia Britannica Online: http://www.britannica.com/EBchecked/topic/185972/emotion

Edelman, G. M. (2004). *Wider than the Sky: a Revolutionary View of Consciousness.* London: Penguin.

Einstein, A. (1970). *Relativity: The Special and the General Theory*. New York: Random House.

free will. (2010). In *Encyclopædia Britannica*. Retrieved 18 January 2010, from Encyclopædia Britannica Online: http://www.britannica.com/EBchecked/topic/218436/free-will

Freud, S. (2009). In *Encyclopædia Britannica*. Retrieved 27 October 2009, from Encyclopædia Britannica Online: http://www.britannica.com/EBchecked/topic/219848/Sigmund-Freud

Glynn, A. (1999). *An Anatomy of Thought: The Origin and Machinery of the Mind*. Oxford: Oxford University Press.

Gopinath, G. (1995). *The Brain: A Precious Possession*. New Dehli: National Books Trust, India.

hallucination. (2009). In *Encyclopædia Britannica*. Retrieved 10 November 2009, from Encyclopædia Britannica Online: http://www.britannica.com/EBchecked/topic/252916/hallucination

Hawking, S. (1988). *A Brief History of Time: From the Big Bang to Black Holes*. Auckland, NZ: Transworld Publishers Ltd.

Hawking, S. & Mlodinow, L. (2010). *The Grand Design*. Johannesburg: Bantam Press.

human nervous system. (2010). In *Encyclopædia Britannica*. Retrieved 4 January 2010, from Encyclopædia Britannica Online: http://www.britannica.com/EBchecked/topic/409709/human-nervous-system

hyperthyroidism. (2009). In *Encyclopædia Britannica*. Retrieved 21 October 2009, from Encyclopædia Britannica Online: http://www. britannica.com/EBchecked/topic/279737/hyperthyroidism

inner ear. (2009). In *Encyclopædia Britannica*. Retrieved 21 October 2009, from Encyclopædia Britannica Online: http://www.britannica.com/ EBchecked/topic/288499/inner-ear

James, W. (2009). In *Encyclopædia Britannica*. Retrieved 20 October 2009, from Encyclopædia Britannica Online: http://www.britannica. com/EBchecked/topic/299871/William-James

James, W. (2009). *Talk to Teachers on Psychology and to Students on Some of Life's Ideals* Ch 12d, http://ebooks.adelaide.edu.au/j/james/william/ talks/complete.html, (eBooks@Adelaide, University of Adelaide, 2009).

Jędrej, M.C., & Shaw, R. (Eds). (1992). *Dreaming, Religion, and Society in Africa*. Leiden, The Netherlands: E.J. Brill.

Jung, C. (2009). In *Encyclopædia Britannica*. Retrieved 10 November 2009, from Encyclopædia Britannica Online: http://www.britannica. com/EBchecked/topic/308188/Carl-Jung

Jung, C. (1983). *Memories, Dreams Reflections*. New York: Flamingo/ Random House

Kornhuber, H. H., & Deecke, L.(1965). Changes in the brain potential in voluntary movements and passive movements in man: readiness potential and reafferent potentials. *Pflugers Arch Gesamte Physiol Menschen Tiere. 10/284*, 1-17.

Libet, B. (1999). Do we have free will? *Journal of Conscious Studies, 6/8-9*, 47-57 (11)

Libet, B., Curtis, A., & Gleason, C. A., Wright, E. W., Pearl, D. K. (1983). Time of conscious intention to act in relation to onset of cerebral activity (readiness potential). *Brain, 106*, 623-642.

Lorenzi, R. *Elephants Mourn Their Dead*, Animal Planet News, Discovery Channel, http://animal.discovery.com/news/briefs/20051031/elephant_02.html

Luria, A. R. (1968/1987). *The Mind of a Mnemonist. A Little Book About a Vast Memory*. Lynn Solotaroff, translator. Cambridge, MA: Harvard University Press.

Marais, E. (1969). *The Soul of the Ape*. Cape Town: Human and Rousseau Publishers Ltd.

Marcus, G. F. (2004). *The Birth of the Mind: How a tiny number of genes creates the complexities of human thought*. New York: Basic Books.

Mirmiran, M. (1995). The function of fetal/neonatal rapid eye movement sleep. *Behavioural Brain Research*, 69, 13-22

mnemonic. (2010). In *Encyclopædia Britannica*. Retrieved 4 January 2010, from Encyclopædia Britannica Online: http://www.britannica.com/EBchecked/topic/386631/mnemonic

Moore, Ruth and the Editors of Life (1964). *Evolution*. (Nederland) NV: Time-Life International.

Nørretranders, T. (1998). *The User Illusion: Cutting Consciousness Down to Size*. London: Penguin.

O'Connor, Timothy, "Free Will", *The Stanford Encyclopedia of Philosophy (Fall 2008 Edition)*, Edward N. Zalta (ed.), URL http://plato.stanford.edu/archives/fall2008/entries/freewill/

Penrose, R. (1995). *Shadows of the Mind*. London: Vintage (Random House).

Pinker, S. (1997). *How the Mind Works*. London: Penguin Books.

play. (2009). In *Encyclopædia Britannica*. Retrieved 21 October 2009, from Encyclopædia Britannica Online: http://www.britannica.com/ EBchecked/topic/464349/play

poker. (2009). In *Encyclopædia Britannica*. Retrieved 21 October 2009, from Encyclopædia Britannica Online: http://www.britannica.com/ EBchecked/topic/466636/poker

premenstrual syndrome (PMS). (2009). In *Encyclopædia Britannica*. Retrieved 21 October 2009, from Encyclopædia Britannica Online: http:// www.britannica.com/EBchecked/topic/474890/premenstrual-syndrome

Rajadhyaksha, M. S. (1996). *The Memory Mystery*. New Dehli: National Books Trust, India.

Ramachandran, V. S., Blakeslee, S. (2005). *Phantoms in the Brain*. London: Harper Perennial.

rapid eye movement sleep. (2009). In *Encyclopædia Britannica*. Retrieved 10 November 2009, from Encyclopædia Britannica Online: http://www. britannica.com/EBchecked/topic/491489/rapid-eye-movement-sleep

Schoeman, P. J. (1963). *Trados die Swerwer-Boesman*. Johannesburg: Voortrekkerpers Ltd.

sleep. (2009). In *Encyclopædia Britannica*. Retrieved 17 November 2009, from Encyclopædia Britannica Online: http://www.britannica.com/ EBchecked/topic/548545/sleep synesthesia. (2010). In *Encyclopædia Britannica*. Retrieved 5 January 2010, from Encyclopædia Britannica Online: http://www.britannica.com/EBchecked/topic/578457/synesthesia

telepathy. (2009). In *Encyclopædia Britannica*. Retrieved 21 October 2009, from Encyclopædia Britannica Online: http://www.britannica.com/EBchecked/topic/585989/telepathy

thermoreception. (2009). In *Encyclopædia Britannica*. Retrieved 21 October 2009, from Encyclopædia Britannica Online: http://www.britannica.com/EBchecked/topic/591718/thermoreception

thermoregulation. (2009). In *Encyclopædia Britannica*. Retrieved 21 October 2009, from Encyclopædia Britannica Online: http://www.britannica.com/EBchecked/topic/591729/thermoregulation

Trimmer, S. M. *How to keep a poker face*, http://www.helium.com/knowledge/47645-how-to-keep-a-poker-face

Watt, S. (Managing Editor). (2002). *Making the Most of your Brain*. London: Duncan Baird Publishers Ltd.

Wegner, D.M. (2002). *The Illusion of Conscious Will*. Cambridge, Massachusetts: Massachusetts Institute of Technology.

Young, R. (1980). *Young's Analytical Concordance to the Bible*. Peabody, Massachusetts: Hendrickson Publishers.

Zimmerman, B. J. & Schunk D. H. (2003).*Educational Psychology: A Century of Contributions* Ch 2, http://www.des.emory.edu/mfp/PajaresJames.PDF, (Lawrence Erlbaum Associates Publishers Mahwah, New Jersey, London, 2003).

About the Author

Anthony Penderis first qualified with an Honours Degree in Civil Engineering before his keen interest in all things human led him to complete courses in a diverse range of subjects such as anatomy, physiology, philosophy, political philosophy, speech and drama, and creative writing. He then turned to journalism and eventually ended up as a Managing Editor for a large publishing house in Dubai. His background uniquely positioned him to produce his theory on the Laws of Thinking, which, in his quest to understand the human mind, he developed over a period of ten years.

He now runs his own media and communications agency and lives in Cape Town, South Africa. See www.anthonypenderis.com.